CW01082676

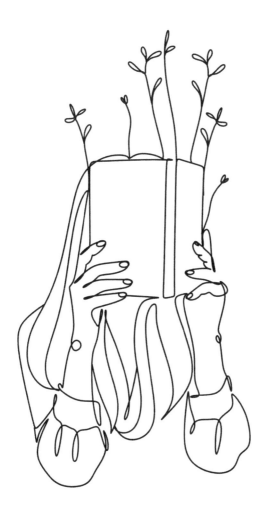

Original title: Soulmate

Author: Liisi Lendorav
Editor: Jessica Elisabeth Luik
ISBN 978-9916-86-004-5

Soulmate

Liisi Lendorav

Sacred Connection

In silence, hearts entwine
Beyond all space and time
A sacred bond, divine
Tethered in endless rhyme

Through storm and clear blue sky
Together, we shall fly
With spirits ever high
Unbroken, we comply

A dance of timeless grace
In love's embrace, we trace
The ancient paths we chase
Two souls, one sacred place

Eternal Whispers

The stars begin to glow
With whispers from below
A language we both know
In twilight's tender show

Through shadows, we will roam
This world we call our home
Where oceans speak in foam
And mountains stand alone

In every breath we take
Eternal vows we make
A bond they cannot break
Together, wide awake

With whispers soft and clear
We banish every fear
Our hearts will persevere
Eternal, year by year

Inseparable Souls

From dawn till dusk we stride
With no mistakes to hide
Our hearts beat side by side
In love, we do abide

Through valleys dark and deep
We share the dreams we keep
In night's enchanting sleep
Our promises we reap

In laughter and in woe
Together we shall grow
In love's eternal glow
Our souls, they always know

Divine Complicity

A secret language shared
In every glance and stare
Our souls are ever paired
Two minds beyond compare

With whispered plans we weave
The story we believe
No room for us to grieve
In us, no force can cleave

Through life's complexities
In divine simplicities
Together, we are free
In cosmic unity

Melodies of Unity

In the chorus of the dawn,
Where night shadows are withdrawn,
Voices blend in harmony,
Crafting love's sweet euphony.

Raindrops join in nature's chord,
Streams of life we all afford,
Tunes of hope in hearts align,
Binding souls in rhythmic time.

From the whispers of the breeze,
To the rustle of the trees,
Symphonies in every heart,
Melodies that never part.

Eternal Dance

Stars cascade in night's embrace,
Lighting up the endless space,
Twinkling lights in cosmic trance,
Join the sky's eternal dance.

Oceans sway with tidal grace,
Moon's soft pull they can't displace,
Waves and winds in perfect tune,
Breathing life beneath the moon.

Mountains rise in silent pride,
Rivers carve their path with stride,
Nature's waltz through time's expanse,
Life partakes in eternal dance.

Unseen Symphony

In the quiet of the mind,
Rhythms unseen we can find,
Thoughts like notes on empty page,
Crafting dreams on life's grand stage.

Eyes may miss what hearts can see,
Motion in tranquility,
Softest whispers, gentlest key,
Play the unseen symphony.

Every heartbeat marks a beat,
In this score so pure and sweet,
Feel the music deep within,
Let your soul's true song begin.

Boundless Affection

In the eyes of lovers' gaze,
Where the world is set ablaze,
Every glance a sweet caress,
Boundless affection we possess.

Hand in hand through stormy night,
Hearts aglow with guiding light,
Souls entwined in love's embrace,
Time and space cannot erase.

Through the laughter, through the tears,
Through the days and through the years,
Love endures with pure protection,
Nurtured by our boundless affection.

Eternal Mingle

In twilight hues, we find our song,
Where day and night embrace the dawn.
The stars above, their light so strong,
Through cosmic dance, we are reborn.

Eclipses form in passion's wake,
A timeless bond, a path we take.
In every glance, our souls partake,
This dance of love shall never break.

Through galaxies, our whispers soar,
Eternal echoes evermore.
Together, drifting to the shore,
Of dreams we've sought and yet explore.

No earthly chain can bind us tight,
In realms untouched by time's cruel might.
We blend as one in endless flight,
Two hearts aglow in the starlit night.

So let us drift, entwined in grace,
Through endless skies, in calm embrace.
Our spirits joined in silent space,
Where time stands still, our sacred place.

Unfading Ties

Beneath the willow, soft and green,
Two hearts entwine like roots unseen.
In whispered winds, our vows convene,
A bond of love, serene, pristine.

Each season paints our canvas bright,
From spring's first bloom to winter's night.
In every storm, in morning light,
Our love remains a steadfast sight.

Though years may pass, and faces change,
Our spirits, close, will never range.
In silken threads, our hopes arrange,
A tapestry that none estrange.

In laughter's realm and sorrow's tide,
Through peaks and valleys, side by side.
Unfading ties, our love and guide,
In every step, our hearts abide.

So let the world, in fleeting stride,
Attempt to pull our hands apart.
For in the depth where dreams reside,
We'll find each other, heart to heart.

Heartstrings Unite

In a dance of fate we met
Strings intertwined with care
Melodies of heartstrings set
A love beyond compare

Whispers in the night
Gentle as a dream
Heartbeats' soft delight
In a star's bright gleam

Together we stand tall
Through the trials we face
Answering love's call
Finding our own place

Bound by threads unseen
Woven deep and tight
In every tender scene
Our heartstrings unite

Forever Two

In the garden where we rove
Hand in hand we stride
A timeless tale of love
In each other's eyes

Sunsets paint the sky
With hues of passion pure
Two souls lifted high
In love that's ever sure

Through the storms outside
Sheltered in embrace
Together we will bide
Time's unyielding pace

For in your heart I find
A universe that's true
Bound in love so kind
Eternally, forever two

Spirit's Twin Flame

Across the astral plane
Our spirits find their mark
Together we'll remain
Bright as the morning spark

In a dance of cosmic fire
Twin flames glowing bright
Rising ever higher
Puring through the night

Boundless in our quest
Through realms far and wide
In each other, find our rest
Our hearts open wide

Unified and whole
In love's eternal game
For you complete my soul
My spirit's twin flame

Love Across Lifetimes

In lives that came before
Our love has always been
Written in the lore
Of epochs we have seen

Through centuries we passed
Our spirits intertwined
A love that ever lasts
Transcending space and time

In dreams, your whisper calls
A voice I've always known
A love that never falls
Forever we'll have grown

Each lifetime we renew
Our souls' eternal chimes
Bound by love so true
Love across lifetimes

Infinite Embrace

In the echoes of the night, we find our place,
Two souls entwined in an infinite embrace.
Stars above whisper secrets in their glow,
Eternal love in the moonlight's soft flow.

Time stands still when we are near,
Boundless love, free from fear.
In every heartbeat, in every sigh,
We float together, you and I.

With every sunrise, a promise anew,
To cherish the bond between me and you.
Rivers of dreams cascade and blend,
Two hearts that time cannot bend.

Divine Synchronicity

In the realm where dreams align,
Fates converge in perfect time.
A dance of souls in harmony,
Crafted by divine synchronicity.

Whispers of the universe, so rare,
Guide our paths with tender care.
Threads of destiny weave us tight,
In the tapestry of love's pure light.

Moments fleeting, yet so vast,
Merge our futures with our past.
Every glance, every touch,
Speaks of a love that means so much.

Parallel Hearts

In worlds apart, we softly tread,
Parallel hearts, by fate led.
Time and space find no divide,
In the love we hold inside.

In silent echoes, our feelings trace,
Two lives entwined, a secret grace.
Through distance vast, our spirits meet,
In a place where dreams are sweet.

Bound by whispers of the unseen,
Separate paths, yet hearts serene.
Eternal is our quiet song,
A love that's sure, enduring strong.

Love's Constellation

Gazing up at cosmic seas,
We find our love among the trees.
Stars arrange a sacred chart,
Mapping journeys of the heart.

In the expanse of twilight skies,
Our love as bright as fireflies.
Each constellation tells our tale,
In love's vast ocean, we set sail.

In whispers of the evening breeze,
We're cradled by celestial ease.
Our hearts align in astral dance,
Bound forever in romance.

Universal Love

Beneath the stars, where dreams unfold,
We find a love both warm and bold,
A bond that stretches far and wide,
Uniting hearts on every side.

In every smile, in every tear,
Shared moments hold us ever near,
A love that echoes through the night,
Guiding souls with gentle light.

From dawn's embrace to twilight's end,
This force of love will never bend,
In cosmic dance, our spirits blend,
To universal love, we all ascend.

Singular Harmony

In the hush of twilight's gleam,
Nature sings a song unseen,
A symphony of lives entwined,
In harmony, our souls aligned.

Each note a whisper, soft and pure,
A melody that will endure,
In every heart, a silent plea,
For singular tranquility.

Through valleys deep and mountains high,
Our voices blend beneath the sky,
A perfect chord, a timeless rhyme,
In harmony, beyond all time.

Spiritual Kinship

In the quiet of the soul's retreat,
We find a kinship, pure and sweet,
A bond that ages cannot break,
In every breath, our spirits wake.

Across the realms of thought and dreams,
A deeper truth in silence gleams,
Connected hearts through space and time,
A union forged, celestial chime.

Through trials faced and burdens shared,
This sacred kinship we have dared,
With hands entwined, we journey far,
Guided by love, our guiding star.

Celestial Companions

Upon the cosmic seas we sail,
With hearts so free, we shall not fail,
Celestial companions, hand in hand,
We travel through this wondrous land.

Each star above, a beacon bright,
Illuminates our path at night,
In galaxy's embrace, so vast,
Together, we shall stand steadfast.

Our spirits whisper, soft and true,
A bond unbroken, ever new,
In every dawn, in every dusk,
Celestial love, our hearts entrust.

Love's Whisper

In the quiet night, your voice, so near
Heartbeats sync in tender cheer
Moonlight dancing, shadows clear
Softly, you whisper, 'I'm always here.'

Under starlit skies, dreams align
Your touch, a promise, pure, divine
Through the winds, our souls entwine
Whispered vows, forever mine.

In dawn's embrace, our hopes arise
Love's whisper, a sweet surprise
Endless echoes, in your eyes
A bond that time never denies.

Eternal Melody

Tunes of love, soft and sweet
In our hearts, the rhythms meet
Every chord, a heartbeat fleet
In your arms, the perfect beat.

Songs of us, beneath the moon
Love's refrain, a timeless tune
Dancing hearts, in perfect swoon
Eternal melody, our boon.

In the symphony of dreams, we play
Notes of love, night and day
Through life's symphony, we sway
Together, forever, come what may.

Love's Sanctuary

A hidden refuge, where hearts reside
In your embrace, our worlds collide
Sheltered dreams, with love as guide
In love's sanctuary, side by side.

Under vaulted skies, we find our peace
Whispers of love, never cease
Within these walls, sweet release
Moments of bliss, joys increase.

In your eyes, a gentle spark
Guiding love, through the dark
In love's sanctuary, no remark
Just our hearts, leaving their mark.

Infinite Bond

Threads of time, woven tight
In love's embrace, endless light
Through the dark, shining bright
Infinite bond, pure and right.

Hearts aligned, paths entwined
Love's journey, undefined
Eternal flame, always kind
Our souls, forever bind.

In every whisper, every glance
Infinite bond, our love's dance
Together, in life's expanse
Endless love, in perfect trance.

Whispers of the Heart

In the quiet of the night,
Where moonlight casts its spell,
Whispers of the heart take flight,
In tales only hearts can tell.

Each beat a story old,
Carved in silence deep,
In dreams our souls enfold,
Through secrets we do keep.

Through shadows love does dance,
A waltz in twilight's glow,
Lost in a fleeting trance,
A whisper none can know.

Where wishes come to pass,
And hopes are gently spun,
Moments in a looking glass,
Where two hearts beat as one.

Endless Connection

Beyond the veil of time,
Where echoes softly blend,
A rhythm pure and prime,
Through ages without end.

Infinite skies we chase,
With stars our guide and friend,
Embraced in endless space,
A bond we can't suspend.

A tether to the soul,
Unseen but ever true,
In every wave and shoal,
Our spirits' endless view.

Crossing realms unseen,
In dreams we find our way,
An endless connection between,
Night, dawn, and day.

Through timeless winds we sail,
In whispers soft and kind,
Together we will prevail,
In heart, in soul, in mind.

Celestial Bond

Among the stars we roam,
Through cosmic tides we sail,
In vast celestial home,
Our journeys never stale.

In orbits we entwine,
Our paths forever linked,
Your light, forever mine,
In constellations inked.

Through nebulae's embrace,
Boundless and untamed,
Every secret space,
With love our hearts have claimed.

With meteors alight,
And comets trailing bright,
We forge our bond in night,
Through every starry flight.

Harmonious Souls

In symphony we meet,
A melody so pure,
Two souls in rhythmic beat,
Eternal and secure.

Our hearts compose a song,
No words can best convey,
A bond so firm and strong,
In harmony we stay.

Through life's alive refrain,
Each note a pledge anew,
In gladness and in pain,
Our symphony is true.

Together we create,
A masterpiece of sound,
Our fates forever mate,
In harmony profound.

As one our spirits rise,
Transcending time and space,
In love that never dies,
A melody of grace.

Celestial Harmony

In a sky where stars align,
Galaxies whisper, planets shine,
Moon and sun in dance divine,
Celestial notes in the ether's wine.

Harmony in spheres afar,
Each a pulse, a vibrant star,
Singing tunes of old and new,
In the cosmos, a timeless view.

Meteors streak across the dark,
Each one leaves a glowing mark,
A cascade of light and dream,
Nature's vast celestial scheme.

Nebulae in colors spread,
Cosmic blooms in astral bed,
Echoes of a silent vow,
In the sky's eternal now.

Listen to the heavens' song,
In their music, we belong,
Infinite and deeply free,
Harmony of galaxy.

Hearts in Orbit

Around and round our souls do spin,
Bound by love, the core within,
Across the void, our hearts find grace,
Orbiting in time and space.

A dance of lights, unseen, yet true,
In pattern set for me and you,
Through cosmic tides and stellar breeze,
Love flows steady, seeks to please.

Gravitational pulls so strong,
To one another we belong,
Each whisper loud, in silence heard,
In our orbit, every word.

Star-crossed paths that intertwine,
Love's vast journey, so divine,
In your eyes, the heavens see,
A universe in you and me.

Eternal flight, our hearts embrace,
In orbiting this sacred space,
Bound no longer by the ground,
To our love, the stars are bound.

Divine Rhythm

In the echo of the dawn,
Where the first light has withdrawn,
Whispers of a world unseen,
In rhythm, the divine convene.

Beats that move the earth and air,
Silent songs both bold and fair,
In this dance, a sacred grace,
Rhythm flows in every place.

Winds in concert with the sea,
Nature's gentle symphony,
Heartbeats timed with lunar phase,
In rhythm, life's eternal praise.

Mountains hum a soundless tune,
Beat of sun and crescent moon,
Every leaf and drop of rain,
Dances in a soft refrain.

Feel the pulse within your soul,
Universe in true control,
Step in time with cosmic hymn,
In the flow, where spirits brim.

Unbreakable Link

In the chain that life does build,
Every link with love instilled,
Unseen forces, strong and sure,
Bind our spirits evermore.

From your heart, a beam of light,
Shines through shadows, piercing night,
Connection steadfast as the sea,
In this link, eternity.

Hand in hand through time we walk,
Silent words our souls do talk,
Courage drawn from ties so deep,
Unbreakable, the bond we keep.

Through the storms and trials faced,
Every challenge we've embraced,
In this weave, so finely spun,
Threads of love bind us as one.

Unseen, but always felt,
In this bond, our spirits melt,
One heart, one beat, one place we'll find,
Unbreakable, by love defined.

Boundless Connection

Whispers of the twilight breeze,
Beneath the canopy of stars,
Hearts entwined in rhythmic ease,
No distance, nor any scars.

In this sacred, silent space,
Souls converse in quiet prose,
Every beat a tight embrace,
Endless is how love grows.

Hand in hand, we tread the night,
Shadows fading, soft and mild,
In the moon's ethereal light,
Dreams and wishes reconciled.

Fusion of the minds and souls,
Breaking boundaries, conquering fears,
In each other, we find our roles,
Transcending days and years.

Sacred Symphony

Melodies that touch the sky,
Harmonies of distant spheres,
Silent notes to amplify,
Chasing echoes of our years.

A chorus of untamed hearts,
Resonates through space and time,
In this symphony, all parts,
Blend in an eternal rhyme.

Celestial chords begin to rise,
Strings of fate both strong and true,
In this song, no love denies,
Life's profound debut.

Each verse a testament of grace,
Lyrics carved in unseen light,
In this sacred, boundless place,
Our spirits take their flight.

Love's Chronos

Minutes turning into days,
Seconds fold like morning dew,
In the clock's unending gaze,
Time reveals its sacred view.

Echoes of a love profound,
Mark the hours, soft and sweet,
In each moment, we are bound,
Chronos makes our hearts complete.

Days unfold like petals wide,
Minutes bloom in subtle grace,
Hand in hand, we walk and bide,
Time our only holy space.

Eternal in this sacred flow,
Chronos bends, our love to see,
In each tick, our feelings grow,
An infinite chronometry.

Timeless Tie

Threads of fate, both fine and strong,
Woven in the loom of life,
Create a bond where we belong,
Beyond the reach of worldly strife.

Tangles in the fabric weave,
Patterns merging in the night,
In our hearts, we won't deceive,
Timeless in our pure delight.

Moments twist and seconds merge,
In this dance of you and I,
Endless waves, a ceaseless surge,
Guided by a timeless tie.

Seasons fade but never part,
In the core of love's embrace,
Joined by strings from heart to heart,
Timeless spans we gently trace.

Eternal Dance

In twilight's soft and golden hue,
Our souls begin their rhythmic flight.
With every step, the old renew,
In this eternal dance of night.

Beneath the stars, our spirits weave,
In cosmic tales of love and lore.
Timeless patterns we believe,
Through endless skies, forevermore.

Whispers of the gentle breeze,
Echoes of the ancient tune.
In perfect harmony, with ease,
We circle 'round the silver moon.

Bound by threads of fate's design,
Our hearts in sync, a sacred trance.
Together, endless we define,
The magic of our timeless dance.

Heart's Mirror

In the quiet of my soul,
Your reflection comes to light.
Where our separate parts are whole,
In the mirror of the night.

Your eyes, they whisper truths untold,
In their depths, a world unfolds.
Every secret that you hold,
In their gaze, my heart enfolds.

Through the glass of time, we peer,
Seeing dreams that wait to break.
In this still and honest mirror,
All the fears and bonds we make.

Hand in hand, we face our selves,
In reflections pure and true.
In this heart's mirror, where love delves,
I see me and I see you.

Destiny's Embrace

Underneath the starlit skies,
We found our paths entwined as one.
Destiny in your eyes,
A journey that has just begun.

With every step, our futures blend,
In this intricate design.
Through twists and turns, around each bend,
Our souls forever intertwine.

Guided by an unseen force,
We navigate through time and space.
Together on this charted course,
In the warmth of destiny's embrace.

Each moment we've been led to here,
Every choice and every chance.
Now in this place, it's crystal clear,
We dance within destiny's trance.

Timeless Connection

Through eons past, our spirits rove,
In every life, we find our place.
An ancient, yet familiar cove,
Where love transcends both time and space.

In silence, words are lesser things,
For it's our hearts that truly speak.
Beneath time's veil, our chorus sings,
In bonds that neither age nor weak.

We meet beyond the years' divide,
In every glance, a story told.
Your presence ever by my side,
A bond unbroken, brave and bold.

In timeless dreams, we find our peace,
No end to tales that we relate.
In connections that will never cease,
Together, we define our fate.

Serenade of Souls

Beneath the willow's ardent shade,
Two figures waltz in twilight's glade.
Their hearts converse in silent speech,
Within a realm words cannot breach.

A moonbeam's kiss, a starlit sigh,
Awake the dreams that never die.
In rapture's arms, their spirits soar,
To realms where love's forevermore.

Whispered winds like lullabies,
Carry secrets through the skies.
Time, a fleeting lover's game,
Knows their love, unstilled, unclaimed.

Veins of gold in night's embrace,
Weave their fates with tender grace.
Each heartbeat, a celestial tune,
A serenade 'neath pale-lit moon.

Bound by Stars

Across the tapestry of night,
Our destinies in constellations light.
Infinite skies, where stories bloom,
We find our path through cosmic gloom.

Ethereal fields of astral glow,
Bind us close where stardust flows.
Galaxies whisper ancient lore,
Of love and hope forevermore.

Celestial dreams in milky streams,
Guide our hearts through cosmic beams.
In the silence between the worlds,
Our loving threads are yet unfurled.

Through the void, our spirits roam,
Together, yet far from home.
In each other's souls, we find,
The constellations of the mind.

Eternal Symphony

In the concert of the stars,
We play our part, no broken bars.
Harmonies of dawn and dusk,
Resonate in bonds of trust.

Notes like whispers on the breeze,
Echo love through ancient trees.
In shadows cast by moonlit beams,
Unfold our intertwined dreams.

Each heartbeat strikes like a drum,
In time with planets' silent hum.
Rhythms of the universe,
Bind us tight, both better and worse.

Together, we compose the song,
Through nights short and mornings long.
A symphony both bold and true,
In every chord, I find you.

Celestial Partners

On the dance floor of the skies,
We twirl beneath the cosmic eyes.
Orbits crossed, our pathways blend,
A waltz where stars begin and end.

With every step, the heavens sway,
Partners in the Milky Way.
Boundless love in twilight's glow,
Guiding us where dreams do flow.

Galactic whispers, soft and clear,
Speak of love that conquers fear.
In the nebulae's embrace,
We find our perfect place.

Infinite as night is vast,
Our souls unite, our shadows cast.
Together, 'neath the astral dome,
We find in each, our cosmic home.

Fated Hearts

In twilight's gentle embrace,
Two wandering souls find home.
Through paths once etched in stars,
Their fated hearts now roam.

In whispered dreams they meet,
Beneath the moon's soft glow.
A love that time cannot defeat,
As seasons come and go.

Their journey laced with magic,
A dance of fates entwined.
In every glance, a story tragic,
Yet love forever kind.

Through shadows, doubts, and fears,
Their hearts, they fiercely guard.
Guided by the ageless years,
Fated hearts, forever starred.

In silence, they breathe as one,
A rhythm pure and true.
For in each other, they have won,
A love both old and new.

Divine Connection

In realms beyond our sight,
Where dreams and fate align,
Two souls ignite, take flight,
In a love, pure, divine.

Through veils of time they trace,
A journey etched in light.
With every touch, a grace,
In heavens, they unite.

No mortal bounds can sever
The tie that holds them near.
A bond that lives forever,
In realms both far and near.

In whispers of the night,
Their hearts converse in song.
A love glowing bright,
As they forever belong.

With eyes that see beyond,
They find their solace there.
A love that's truly fond,
In the divine, they share.

Radiant Hearts

Beneath the gilded dawn,
Two radiant hearts arise.
In each breath, battles won,
Their love never disguised.

In every laugh and tear,
A luminous embrace.
Through every passing year,
Their love, in light, they trace.

Their joy, the sun, it mirrors,
Their sorrow, shadows cast.
Together, facing fears,
Their love, forever vast.

Through valleys deep and wide,
And peaks that touch the sky,
Their hearts in rhythm glide,
As endless moments fly.

With every pulse, they shine,
A beacon in the night.
In love, they intertwine,
Two hearts, forever bright.

Love's Compass

In the wilderness of time,
Where paths are seldom clear,
Love's compass guides, sublime,
Through every doubt and fear.

With stars as ancient guides,
They find their destined course.
In each other's hearts, abides
An everlasting force.

No matter storms or trials,
Their compass points to love.
With every step, they smile,
Blessed by the stars above.

Through rivers deep and wild,
And deserts yearning wide,
Love's compass, never riled,
Keeps them side by side.

In journeys long and vast,
Their hearts, they navigate.
For in love's compass, cast
Is their eternal fate.

Spirit's Dance

Whispers of wind in twilight's trance
Mystic figures in rhythmic prance
Moonlight caresses the silent land
While spirits sway hand in hand

Ghostly murmurs in forests deep
Their secret tales the night does keep
Glimmer of stars in the boundless sky
Reflects in the spirits' ethereal eye

In shadows where dreams come to play
Phantoms waltz, then fade away
Bound by neither time nor space
In their dance, they find grace

Beneath the canopy of ancient trees
Spirits twirl with perfect ease
Rhapsody of the unseen begins
Blending with the night's soft whispers and grins

Keepers of myths in the midnight hour
Drawn to the dance by hidden power
Their footsteps leave no trace nor sound
In the spirit's dance, they're forever unbound

Eternal Light

In the cradle of the rising dawn
A promise of hope is newly born
Golden beams pierce the morning haze
Guiding hearts through life's winding maze

Through storms and shadows, fierce and high
Eternal light, it does not shy
Beacon of warmth, a guiding star
Steering ships from reefs afar

Brighter than the darkest night
It holds the world in tender light
Shining through the thickest veil
In sacred whispers, it tells its tale

Old as time, yet fresh and pure
Eternal light, timeless allure
Binds the past with futures bright
In its glow, wrongs turn right

With every breath, with every glance
We find solace in its dance
In fields of grey, a vibrant hue
Eternal light, forever true

Celestial Duet

Beneath the vaulted sky so wide
Two stars in night's eternal tide
Dancing through the cosmic sea
In silent, graceful revelry

Their twinkle tells of ancient lore
Of galaxies and spaces more
Ebb and flow in time's own thread
In their light, dreams are fed

Through the vast expanse, they speak
In languages of light they seek
To bridge the gap, from near to far
Symbols drawn by stellar bar

In this duet, a harmony
Of beauty, love, and mystery
Two points of light in perfect tune
Forever sing beneath the moon

Guiding souls with gentle beams
Celestial kin in shared dreams
They waltz above, so pure, so free
In endless cosmic symphony

Infinite Rhythms

In the pulse of the morning heart
Life awakens with a start
Echoes from the dawn of time
Blend with nature's gentle chime

Rhythms in the rustling leaves
In every breath the forest breathes
Streams that weave a song so sweet
In their dance, earth and sky meet

From the flutter of a butterfly
To the thunder rolling by
Symphony of the raw and wild
In infinite rhythms, undefiled

Beats of life in every form
In fragile leaves, in brewing storm
Unified in nature's play
An eternal, vibrant ballet

In the heartbeat of the oceans deep
In every dream we dare to keep
Infinite rhythms, softly play
In every dawn, in every day

Spirit's Pilgrimage

In twilight's hush, the journey starts,
A whisper calls from distant lands.
Through valleys deep, o'er mountains high,
The spirit braves, with unseen hands.

With each footfall, a story told,
In realms where shadows dance and fade.
The heart beats on, in quest of dreams,
Bound to a path by fate displayed.

In fleeting moments, landscapes shift,
Stars align, yet time stands still.
The wanderer finds solace there,
Amidst the calm, on twilight's hill.

Through storm and calm, the spirit flies,
Unfurling wings beneath the sky.
Boundless realms in sight ahead,
Seeking truths where secrets lie.

At journey's end, a light reveals,
The soul's reflection in divine.
In every step, the spirit grows,
Completing paths in endless line.

Eternal Melody

In dawn's first light, the song begins,
A melody both old and new.
The notes entwine in harmony,
A timeless tune the world flows through.

With morning's rise, the chorus swells,
Nature's voice in perfect pitch.
Each whispering leaf and sighing wind,
Creates a symphony, rich.

By noon's high sun, the song persists,
A lyric borne of earth and sky.
Harmonizing life's sweet breath,
An endless hymn as moments fly.

At twilight's end, the echoes fade,
Yet still the tune's soft rhythm stays.
Through dreams it weaves its gentle spell,
A lullaby of bygone days.

In every heart, the melody rings,
An eternal song without cease.
A cadence of the universe,
In perfect bliss, in perfect peace.

Yoked Eternities

In stardust thread, the cosmos weave,
Two destinies in shadow's dance.
Linked by an ancient, unseen bond,
Entwined through time in chance.

From birth in stars to life below,
Their paths converge in silent grace.
Through epochs lost and future dreams,
Together, they find their place.

In whispered winds and silent nights,
Their spirits merge, where worlds divide.
For in the heart of deepest dark,
Their lights as one, forever guide.

Though time may twist and space may part,
Their souls remain in unity.
For every breath and heartbeat shared,
Proclaims their yoked eternity.

In final dawn, when time stands still,
They face the stars, forever bright.
Hand in hand, as one they walk,
Into the boundless light.

Heart's Home

Through forests dense and meadows green,
The heart seeks out its place of rest.
In quiet glades where echoes fade,
It finds the peace within its chest.

Beneath the sky, both vast and blue,
Among the stars' celestial dome,
The soul feels drawn to kindred lands,
A place it knows, its ancient home.

In whispers soft, the mountains speak,
Their silent tales of ages old.
The rivers sing in crystal notes,
Of journeys past and wings of gold.

Amidst the fields where wildflowers bloom,
The heart discovers solace true.
It rests in nature's warm embrace,
In every breath, in morning dew.

And when the twilight claims the day,
Under moon's soft, tender glow,
The heart finds home in loving arms,
Where truth and love eternally flow.

Celestial Threads

In heavens high, where starlight weaves,
Beyond the moon, where shadows cleave,
Threads of gold and silver breeze,
Bind the cosmos in silent ease.

Ancient galaxies twirl and sway,
In a dance that night won't betray,
Through celestial threads, they convey,
Whispers of a distant day.

Nebulae bloom in colors bright,
Comets carve the darkest night,
Ever intertwined in flight,
Guided by a hidden light.

A tapestry of endless sky,
Maps the realms where spirits fly,
Woven tight where dreams rely,
On threads no mortal can untie.

As dawn ascends, the patterns fade,
Yet in our hearts, the echoes stayed,
Of celestial threads, finely laid,
In the silent night, where they played.

Unseen Bonds

Invisible lines connect our souls,
Stronger than iron, gentle as coals,
Woven where no eye consoles,
The unseen bonds that make us whole.

In whispers soft, our hearts align,
Bound by threads no fate maligns,
In secret glances, signals find,
The unseen bonds, by love defined.

Through trials faced and joys we share,
In silent prayers, and dreams laid bare,
Invisible, yet always there,
Unseen bonds show we truly care.

In moments when we drift apart,
These bonds remind, soul to heart,
Distance cannot tear the chart,
Of unseen bonds that never depart.

In the quiet, they hold us tight,
Threads of love, in shadowed light,
Anchoring us through day and night,
Unseen bonds, forever in sight.

Ethereal Love

In realms where dreams and shadows lie,
Lives a love that never dies,
Ethereal, untouched by sighs,
Soft and pure, like twilight skies.

In whispers carried by the breeze,
In the rustle of the trees,
Love's essence flows with ease,
Ethereal, meant to please.

No boundaries can this love restrain,
It dances in the gentle rain,
In every joy and subtle pain,
Ethereal love, without disdain.

Through time and space it finds its way,
In moonlit nights and brightened day,
In every heart, it wishes stay,
Ethereal love, forever in play.

A bond that knows no earthly bind,
In the soul and purest mind,
Eternal, gentle, intertwined,
Ethereal love, divinely designed.

Timeless Echoes

Through valleys deep and mountains high,
Across the rivers, through the sky,
Timeless echoes softly sigh,
Of memories that defy goodbye.

In ancient stones and whispered tales,
In morning mists, and wind's light wails,
Time unravels, yet prevails,
In echoes where the past unveils.

In hearts that beat with shared refrain,
In tears and laughter, joy, and pain,
Timeless echoes still remain,
Binding spirits with unseen chain.

In moments fleeting, life unfolds,
Through timeless echoes, truth behold,
The stories that our fates have told,
Glimmer through the ages, bold.

Eternal whispers, soft and clear,
Of love and loss, of hope and fear,
Timeless echoes always near,
A symphony for all who hear.

Love's Destiny

In the whisper of the twilight breeze,
A promise emerges, soft and true,
Carrying dreams across the seas,
With destinies crafted anew.

Stars align in silent grace,
Guiding hearts to a destined shore,
Fate and love, in a tender embrace,
Two souls meet, and journey once more.

Every glance, a timeless story told,
In a dance of fate and desire,
A love that neither time can hold,
Nor weary paths ever tire.

Bound by strings unseen and fine,
Hearts wander, yet always find,
A destiny that intertwines,
Love's path, endlessly kind.

As dawn breaks through the night,
Their souls in unity withstand,
Love's destiny shines so bright,
Two hearts forever hand-in-hand.

Harmonious Souls

In the cadence of a gentle stream,
Two hearts find melodies sweet,
Blending notes like a dream,
In harmony, where spirits meet.

Moments drift on feathered kisses,
Silent songs only hearts compose,
Binding vows life never dismisses,
A symphony that endlessly grows.

Each whisper, a tender refrain,
Echoing in chambers deep,
Two souls, unchained by refrain,
In harmony, their secrets keep.

The world may leap and sway,
But their song remains pristine,
A love that cannot decay,
In harmony, serene and keen.

Thus, they dance to love's sweet tune,
With each note, their souls align,
Under the silvery glow of the moon,
In harmony, forever they shine.

Timeless Spirits

Across the sands of untamed time,
Two spirits weave a hallowed tale,
In realms where love and fate rhyme,
Their essence, an eternal veil.

Each moment shared, a timeless spark,
Lighting paths in twilight mist,
Guiding through the unknown dark,
Where love's gentle winds persist.

Memories carved in ancient stone,
Whisper tales of hearts so brave,
Their spirits never are alone,
In love's embrace, they forever lave.

In dreams where echoes softly glide,
Time bows to the ageless song,
Spirits bound, they side by side,
Face the world's ceaseless throng.

And when the stars their chapters close,
In the sky of endless blue,
Timeless spirits, they still compose,
Love's eternal, endless view.

Hearts Aligned

Under skies vast and wide,
Two hearts draw towards the light,
In a world where hopes reside,
They find solace in the night.

Dreams entwine in endless dance,
With steps guided by fate's hand,
Chance and destiny enhance,
Their love's path across the land.

Eyes that speak in silence deep,
Whispers lost in tender air,
Heartbeats in rhythm keep,
A love that's always fair.

Stars above, they softly sing,
Of two souls in perfect tune,
Every dusk and dawn they bring,
A love that waxes with the moon.

With every breath, each touch refined,
Their spirits and hearts realigned,
In the world both bright and kind,
Together, forever intertwined.

Infinite Reflection

Endless mirrors align, dreams they unfold,
Glinting truths in silver, stories retold.
Adrift in echoes, a soul's own reticence,
Infinite windows, boundless reverence.

Light bends 'round corners, a cosmic ballet,
Physics of thoughts in disarray.
Fractal dimensions in every glance,
Universe twinkles, in perpetual dance.

Chaos in clarity, symmetry's kin,
Reflections mirror the world within.
In every shard, a vision so bright,
Eternity captured, in captured light.

Labyrinths wander, in glass they speak,
Secrets whispered, none too oblique.
Silent orators of past's reflection,
Guardians of infinite introspection.

In each reflection, a portal profound,
Echoes of forever, silently sound.
Between the frames, time suspends,
Endless reflections, as the world bends.

Heartfelt Chords

Strings gently strum, emotions unfold,
Stories of love, in melodies told.
Whispers of heartbeats, a symphony sweet,
Harmony dances, where kindred souls meet.

Voices uplifted, in passionate song,
Notes that have waited, for love's lifelong.
Echoes of moments, in perfect tune,
Under the silver, the glimmer of moon.

Chords of affection, softly they ring,
Memories linger, in every string.
An opus of whispers, a heart's own refrain,
Carried by the wind, through joy and through pain.

Melodies weave, a tapestry bright,
Woven with threads of shadow and light.
Songs of the ancients, forever they hum,
In the silence between, where feelings come.

In the cadence of love, time stands still,
Endless refrain, a soul's deepest thrill.
Heartfelt chords, eternally sing,
A testament to love's undying spring.

Unseen Affinity

Invisible threads, binding us tight,
Feeling your presence, out of sight.
Silent whispers, touch so pure,
Unseen affinity, forever sure.

Eyes may not meet, worlds away,
Yet in the silence, we still convey.
Unfurling emotions, silent plea,
Ethereal bond, 'twixt you and me.

Hearts beat as one, no need for light,
A connection intense, beyond sight.
Subtle interactions, unspoken ties,
In dusk and dawn, love never lies.

Through time's fabric, our spirits dance,
Guided by fate, not by chance.
In every heartbeat, in every sigh,
Unseen affinity, reaches the sky.

Mysterious, eternal, bond so rare,
Embracing tightly, through whispered air.
Invisible threads, love's decree,
Bound in spirit, wild and free.

Timeless Union

In ancient stars, our love is writ,
Through epochs vast, it softly lit.
Timeless union, forever endeared,
With every heartbeat, endlessly steered.

Seasons may change, rivers may flow,
Yet together, eternally we grow.
In every moment, timelessly spun,
Two souls united, two become one.

Mountains may crumble, oceans may part,
Still, we remain, heart-to-heart.
Infinity dances, in our embrace,
Time bends to love, finds its place.

Bound by destinies, intertwined,
A covenant sacred, ever aligned.
In each heartbeat, in every breath,
We transcend life, we conquer death.

Timeless union, a song of old,
In love's warm arms, we forever hold.
Through endless ages, dance in delight,
Eternal romance, under starry night.

Unspoken Bond

Eyes that meet in silent grace,
A tethered heart with gentle embrace.
Words unuttered, yet understood,
Echoes of a love that's good.

Hands that brush, a spark ignites,
In quiet glances, our soul alights.
Silent whispers, deep and fond,
We share our unspoken bond.

In moonlit nights, where shadows fall,
Our hearts converse, no need to call.
In the space where silence roams,
We find each other, we find home.

Boundless trust in wordless vows,
A sacred bond that time allows.
In the stillness, love is shown,
In this silence, we're not alone.

Without a sound, our love conveys,
In every look, in myriad ways.
In this tranquil, profound pond,
We swim, forever unspoken bond.

Infinite Affinity

Beyond the stars in the cosmic sea,
Lies a bond of infinite affinity.
In endless realms where dreams reside,
We journey forth, hearts open wide.

In every breath, a promise kept;
Through countless nights where longing slept.
Eternal flames that never die,
We soar together, you and I.

Our souls entwined in fateful dance,
Transcending time by loving chance.
In whispers soft, infinity sings,
Of boundless love and timeless wings.

Through joy and sorrow, all we face,
We find in each a tender grace.
In every heartbeat, love's decree,
Our bond remains, infinitely.

Side by side, through space and time,
We weave our love in endless rhyme.
In universe so vast, so free,
We cherish our infinite affinity.

Hearts Entwined

In twilight's glow, our shadows meet,
Two hearts entwined in rhythmic beat.
Together through the night we weave,
A tapestry of dreams reprieve.

Hand in hand, through storm and sun,
Our journey shared, our hearts as one.
United by a bond so pure,
Through love's embrace, we find our cure.

On paths uncharted, side by side,
In you, my love, I do confide.
With every step, our spirits meld,
In endless love, our hearts are held.

As seasons change, our love remains,
In joy and sorrow, bliss and pains.
For in your eyes, my soul does find,
A home within your heart, entwined.

With gentle whispers, tender kiss,
We find in love our boundless bliss.
Through every tear and laugh combined,
Forevermore, our hearts entwined.

Cosmic Love

In realms beyond the earthly plane,
A cosmic love that breaks the chain.
Through galaxies and stars afar,
We dance beneath a brilliant star.

Celestial motions guide our way,
In endless night and brightest day.
The universe in love conspires,
To fuel our hearts with boundless fires.

In cosmic winds, our spirits soar,
Through astral dreams and comet's roar.
Amongst the nebula, we find,
A love that's vast, a frame of mind.

Infinite skies with constellations,
Our love's the finest of creations.
In every twinkling starry guise,
We see our love through heaven's eyes.

Eternal bonds in cosmic dance,
A love that spans each circumstance.
In realms unknown, our spirits move,
United in this cosmic love.

Unseen Harmony

Whispers on the wind, silent and pure,
In unvoiced symphonies, we find our cure.
In shadows and light, a dance unfolds,
Unseen harmony, a story retold.

The stars in their silent dialogue,
Paint dreams in the sky, a cosmic monologue.
Though eyes may wonder, hearts always see,
The beauty in life's quiet decree.

Soft murmurs of leaves, a hymn unknown,
Nature's verse, on breezes grown.
Invisible threads, they sew and bind,
A tapestry that's one of a kind.

Heartstrings of Fate

In the loom of time, threads intertwine,
Destinies written in patterns fine.
Where hearts are bound, no force can sever,
Heartstrings of fate, enduring forever.

Twists and turns in life's grand play,
Love's compass guides us, come what may.
Each moment passes, a stitch in space,
Binding us together in an infinite embrace.

Fate's needle moves with unseen hands,
Stitching stories across distant lands.
Through trials and hopes, we walk the line,
Interwoven destinies in perfect design.

Cosmic Lullaby

Stars whisper secrets to the night,
In lullabies of ancient light.
Galaxies spin in silent song,
A cosmic lullaby, all night long.

In the velvet sky, dreams take flight,
Guided by the moon's soft light.
Eternal melodies of the stars above,
Serenade the world in cosmic love.

The universe hums a tender tune,
Underneath a watchful moon.
Resting hearts in starlit skies,
Cradled by the night's sweet lullabies.

Eternal Embrace

In the silence of the twilight hour,
Love blooms in a hidden bower.
An eternal embrace, so warm and true,
Binding souls in a timeless hue.

Through trials faced and paths unknown,
Two hearts find strength, overthrown.
In the quiet moments, deep and still,
Love's eternal embrace fulfills.

As the sun and moon exchange their bow,
Promises whispered, spoken vow.
In every heartbeat, love's grace,
An everlasting, eternal embrace.

Eternal Mirror

In the stillness of the glass
Reflections speak of days gone by
Silent whispers from the past
Meet the future in the eye

Bronze and silver intertwine
In a dance that time repeats
Echoes linger, intertwine
In the mirror, fate completes

Glimmers of what once was dear
Fade into a clouded mist
Yet in every falling tear
Lies a hope, a fleeting kiss

In its depth, the world is cast
Fragments of the soul's veneer
Stories told and futures past
In the vision, crystal clear

Each new moment finds its place
In the reflex of forever
Time and stillness interlace
Eternal mirror, ever clever

Heavenly Partners

Beneath a canopy of stars
Two kindred souls take flight
Their whispers travel near and far
Through constellations bright

Dancing on celestial beams
In rhythm with the night
Their laughter threads through silent dreams
Forming bonds so tight

Across the endless velvet sky
In tandem they will soar
Heavenly partners ever nigh
Forever seeking more

Through the galaxies they glide
A cosmic waltz in space
Bound by love, forever tied
In an endless, sweet embrace

No distance can displace their hearts
Nor time erase their song
For in these endless astral charts
Their love remains strong

Kindred Frequencies

On waves of unseen energy
Two spirits find their tune
In harmony of mystery
They sing beneath the moon

Vibrations of a kindred thread
Resonate in silence pure
Their melodies in sync are led
By a force that will endure

A symphony of kindred cords
Flows between their hearts
Invisible yet firm as swords
The music never parts

Through the ether's vast expanse
Their frequencies align
In each beat, a cosmic dance
So vividly divine

In this realm of soundless grace
Their souls forever blend
Kindred frequencies embrace
In tune until the end

Eternal Embrace

Through lifetimes stretching endless, wide
Their arms always entwine
In realms where spirits softly bide
Love's patterns they define

Beneath the sun, the moon, the stars
Their hearts forever meet
Transcending all the ages' scars
In rhythm, pure and sweet

Seasons turn like whispered dreams
Yet constants never fade
In their embrace, the softest beams
Of light and love displayed

Across the sands of time they move
In dance of endless grace
Each moment, tenderly they prove
Their everlasting place

For love that time cannot erase
Lives in every tender trace
Two souls bound in life's embrace
Eternal, face to face

Intertwined Fates

Two lives weave a single thread,
Paths converging, journeys led,
By stars above and unseen hands,
Through unknown lands, united stands.

In twilight's glow, their shadows merge,
Bound by fate, they onward surge,
With whispered dreams, and hopes they share,
A tapestry beyond compare.

In laughter's echo, in tears and smiles,
They travel vast, uncharted miles,
Together strong, through night and day,
In destiny's dance, they sway.

Mountains high and valleys deep,
In hearts they trust, in faith they keep,
Intertwined through seasons' grace,
In each other, they find their place.

For love's a path both rough and sweet,
Where two fates, as one, meet,
In every moment, tender, true,
Their story written, always new.

Harmonizing Hearts

Beats align in perfect time,
In a love that feels sublime,
Songs they sing without refrain,
In sunshine, storm, in joy, in pain.

Their melodies, a soothing rain,
Together they begin again,
No sweeter sound than hearts in tune,
A symphony beneath the moon.

In every note and silent pause,
They understand without a cause,
With every chord, in light and dark,
They share one soul, one vital spark.

Love's duet, in highs and lows,
Harmonies where courage grows,
In unison, they rise and fall,
Their hearts create a thrilling call.

In concert halls or whispered night,
They find their peace, their pure delight,
For in each other, strength and art,
Through life they go, hearts never part.

Dual Radiance

Two stars alight within the night,
Their brilliance casts a shared light,
Across the skies, they boldly trail,
In tandem, through the cosmic veil.

They shine as one, yet deep within,
Dual flames where dreams begin,
In their glow, the darkness fades,
A radiant dance the heavens made.

Celestial paths they intertwine,
Each orbit, a design divine,
Eternal beams in vast expanse,
Together, they in beauty dance.

With every pulse, a world ignites,
In union, they defy the nights,
A treasure trove of luminous grace,
Their glow, a kiss in boundless space.

Two spirits born in starry gleam,
They chase the endless cosmic dream,
In their shine, a love so grand,
Two radiances, hand in hand.

Symbiotic Spirits

In silent languages they speak,
Two souls entwined, both strong and meek,
A bond unseen, yet deeply known,
In each other's essence shown.

As rivers flow to meet the sea,
They journey forth as one, yet free,
In tangled roots, their strength is found,
Together on this fertile ground.

No need for words, for touch, for sight,
Their spirits sense the boundless light,
In every breath, in every sigh,
They lift each other to the sky.

Through storm and calm, through ebb and flow,
Their union helps them rise and grow,
Symbiotic in every way,
They share the dawn of each new day.

Through life's great tapestry they weave,
In love, in trust, they both believe,
For in each other, true and whole,
They find their one, united soul.

Stargazer's Dream

In night's embrace I cast my eyes
To constellations, vast and free
A universe in whispered sighs
Unfolds its ancient tapestry

The stars ignite in endless streams
Each twinkle tells a tale unknown
Within this realm of silent beams
I find a peace I've never known

Galaxies weave through space's seam
A dance that spans eternity
In this celestial, tranquil dream
Discover truths that set me free

The moon a guardian softly glows
A beacon through the cosmic sea
In stillness, secrets it bestows
Upon the heart that's meant to see

My soul entwined with stellar light
In reverie, horizons gleam
Through endless night and boundless sight
I dwell within the stargazer's dream

Love's Nexus

Two hearts converge in tender grace
Where whispers blend in harmony
A single touch, a soft embrace
Defines the bond of you and me

Eclipsing all, this sacred space
Where souls entwine in perfect sync
Within the light of love's warm face
Eternity exists in blink

Through trials faced and moments sweet
Our spirits find a common ground
In every joy and sorrow meet
A love profound, forever bound

With you, the world becomes a song
Composed of whispers, sighs, and dreams
Together, we are ever strong
Uniting streams of life's bright beams

In every heartbeat, call we send
A symphony of love extends
Through time and space, our paths descend
Where love's divine essence transcends

Timeless Bind

Through winds of time, our spirits rise
In moments gone, our echoes chime
Across the ages, endless ties
Entwine our destinies in rhyme

In shadows cast by years gone by
The phantom touch of memories
Through every tear and whispered sigh
A boundless love defies the seas

We've walked through eras hand in hand
Each lifetime yet to understand
A love that spans from land to land
Resilient through the shifting sand

The past, the future, and today
In cyclic paths our souls align
This timeless bind shall light the way
A beacon through the vast design

In dreams and wake, our spirits find
The ancient threads of fate unwind
A love eternal, heart combined
Within this soul's eternal bind

Spirit's Keeper

Within the hush of twilight's veil
I seek the whispers, spirit's song
In shadows deep, where secrets pale
I find where heart and soul belong

The forest breathes with ancient lore
Its trees hold tales of history
A keeper of the spirits' core
A guide into life's mystery

Among the leaves, my spirit soars
In cadence with the wind's embrace
In nature's hymn, my heart explores
Experiencing the sacred grace

In solitude, a wisdom grows
Transcending time's relentless fleet
Where rivers flow and stillness shows
Connection to the earth complete

I am a vessel, tuned to light
A guardian of the spirit's truth
In nature's arms, my soul takes flight
And finds eternal, endless youth

Eternal Echoes

Across the ages, whispers flow,
In hidden realms, where secrets glow,
A timeless dance, where shadows play,
In silent murmurs, night and day.

The echoes rise, and gently fade,
In twilight's grasp, where dreams are made,
Through crystal skies, in realms unknown,
A symphony of ages grown.

In endless loops, they intertwine,
The past and future, bold design,
An ancient chord, forever cast,
In sacred echoes, truths amassed.

From stardust born, to cosmic seas,
A harmony in worlds that freeze,
Their journey's trail, an endless thread,
In every heartbeat, softly spread.

Eternal whispers, calling forth,
In worlds above, and deep in earth,
Their song remains, forever grand,
Eternal echoes, hand in hand.

Heart's Resonance

In melodies of tender grace,
A rhythm found in every space,
The heart's pure song, both near and far,
A guiding light, our constant star.

As days unfold in gentle waves,
It murmurs softly, always saves,
A cadence true, in darkest night,
The heart's resonance, shining bright.

Through endless trials, pain and joy,
Its symphony will never cloy,
A beat that rises, bold and strong,
In every soul, where dreams belong.

With every whisper, pulse, and sigh,
It tells the tales of you and I,
The ancient bonds, no time can break,
In heart's resonance, both wake.

So listen close, and feel the sound,
In every heartbeat, wisdom found,
A song that binds, and never parts,
The resonance of kindred hearts.

Twin Flames

In realms unseen, where shadows meet,
Two flames arise, in heart's own beat,
A mirror's dance, in perfect light,
Eternal bonds, in darkest night.

Their spirits bound, through time and space,
In every touch, a soft embrace,
A fire's glow, in souls conjoined,
In every breath, their love enshrined.

Like destinies, forever twined,
Two hearts as one, in love aligned,
A burning grace, that lights their way,
In twin flames' dance, come what may.

Through trials vast, they stand as one,
Their burning hearts, like brightest sun,
A flicker never shall it cease,
In twin flames' bond, complete release.

In every lifetime, they will find,
The sacred love, so pure, refined,
For they are bound, in soul and name,
Eternal light, in twin flames' flame.

Kindred Spirits

In whispered dawn, where spirits weave,
A bond of light, we can't conceive,
Their paths entwined, in fate's sweet call,
Two kindred hearts, where shadows fall.

Through realms of dreams, their spirits soar,
In every touch, they find the core,
A silent vow, in every glance,
Through life's own dance, a second chance.

In every laugh, in every tear,
Their souls align, in tender sphere,
A kindred bond, that time can't bind,
Eternal love, so deeply kind.

Through trials faced, and joys embraced,
Their spirits soar in endless space,
For they are one, and always near,
In kindred hearts, they persevere.

So let them dance, and let them sing,
In every life, their love will spring,
A timeless bond, forever writ,
In kindred spirits, they commit.

Celestial Romance

Under stars, our hearts entwine,
Twinkling lights, love Divine.
Whispers float, through the night,
In the cosmos, pure delight.

Galaxies paint skyward dreams,
Solitude in moonlit beams.
Mystic rhythms, cosmic dance,
In this realm, love's expanse.

Comets pass, a fleeting kiss,
In the heavens, boundless bliss.
Orbits cross, destinies bind,
In this love, solace find.

Nebulas in hues of blue,
I surrender all to you.
Astral paths, fate's embrace,
In your eyes, endless grace.

Celestial love, timeless flight,
Guided by the Northern Light.
Eternal bond, through the stars,
In your love, no more scars.

Kindred Spirits

In a world of whispered dreams,
Where streams and sunlight seem.
Two hearts brush, a soft caress,
A timeless bond, wordless confess.

Paths converge beneath grand skies,
Echoes of the ancient ties.
Soul and spirit intertwine,
In your eyes, a love divine.

Laughter shared by warming fire,
Heartbeats matching, pure desire.
Through life's maze, hand in hand,
In togetherness, we stand.

Silent promises we keep,
Dreams awaken from their sleep.
Unseen threads, entwine our fate,
In this bond, we celebrate.

Against all odds, side by side,
Storms we weather, ebbing tide.
Kindred spirits, bound by grace,
In your love, I find my place.

Dream Weaver

In the tapestry of night,
You weave dreams, pure delight.
Threads of silver, strands of gold,
Mystic visions, stories told.

Through the realms of slumber deep,
Secrets whispered while we sleep.
From your loom, dreams take flight,
Into worlds of endless light.

Gossamer wings, fairies glide,
In your hands, dreams abide.
Stars align, fables spin,
New dimensions, souls begin.

In your art, the night transforms,
Magic in its myriad forms.
Wonders flow from heart and mind,
In your dreams, solace find.

Dream Weaver, night's embrace,
Crafting dreams with tender grace.
In your realm, dreams unfold,
Forever young, forever bold.

Love's Echo

Softly spoken, love's first sound,
In your heart, echoes found.
Rippled whispers, tender tones,
Love's refrain, in whispered moans.

In the stillness, hearts collide,
In your gaze, worlds reside.
Gentle echoes, softly sway,
Night and day, love's relay.

Mountains high and valleys deep,
Love's echo in the realms we keep.
Through life's journey, paths we trace,
In your love, a dwelling place.

Words unspoken, silent vow,
Love's echo in the here and now.
Timeless rhythm, endless flow,
In your arms, peace we know.

With each heartbeat, echoes blend,
Love's refrain knows no end.
In your presence, life's true glow,
Love's echo, ever so.

Unbreakable Ties

In the whispers of the night,
Bonds that silently align,
Unseen yet shining bright,
Heartstrings that intertwine.

Across miles they connect,
With no need for words spoken,
Through every joy and regret,
Unbreakable, unbroken.

Souls drawn to a common song,
Harmonizing, pure and true,
Ties that forever belong,
Eternal in their hue.

An orchestra of hearts,
In rhythm, in perfect dance,
No distance can keep apart,
This celestial romance.

For in each beat and sigh,
Lives a promise unforgotten,
Unbreakable ties that lie,
In love's binding, begotten.

Invisible Threads

Beneath the gaze of the moon,
Threads of fate quietly weave,
Connecting hearts too soon,
With destinies they believe.

Invisible yet so real,
In the silence, strongly hold,
Every touch, every feel,
A story subtly told.

Whispers in the breeze,
Messages sent afar,
Caught between the leaves,
Guided by the stars.

An unseen force at play,
Binding hearts without tether,
Guiding every day,
With threads that last forever.

So they wander and roam,
In life's intricate web,
Yet find their way home,
To the threads they embed.

Kindred Destinies

We journey through the night,
Stars whisper secrets cold,
Kindred souls take flight,
Destinies to unfold.

In every twist and turn,
Their paths forever meet,
In passion they will burn,
Their fates a rhythmic beat.

Through time and space they roam,
In search of dreams so true,
The heavens are their home,
Their hearts, the compass blue.

Beliefs that never waver,
In shadows light is found,
A destiny to savor,
In love eternally bound.

When morning light will break,
And destiny is shown,
Kindred hearts awake,
Forever not alone.

Cosmic Alignment

Stars are born in skies so vast,
In a dance of purest night,
Aligning futures against the past,
In beams of guiding light.

Planets whisper ancient tales,
Of destinies foretold,
In the quiet of cosmic trails,
A journey to behold.

Galaxies in their embrace,
Harmonize with grace,
Lives converge in sacred space,
A divine, celestial trace.

In the vastness of the above,
Resonates a silent song,
Of endless worlds and boundless love,
Where every soul belongs.

Cosmic forces gently steer,
Hearts to paths aligned,
In the universe so clear,
Their fates intricately designed.

Cosmic Hearts

In the void where stars align,
Two hearts weave through space divine,
Galaxies turn with love, sincere,
Their orbits bound, forever near.

Nebulas paint their endless dream,
Through cosmic winds, they gently stream,
A dance of light in astral skies,
Their pulse, the universe complies.

Through asteroids and comets' flight,
They traverse night, a blazing sight,
In shadows cast by moonlit beams,
Eternal their celestial schemes.

No black hole dims their fervent glow,
Together they eternally flow,
An endless tale of starry art,
The timeless bond of cosmic hearts.

Eternal Flame

A candle burns with steady glow,
Through time and tears, its light does show,
The warmth it brings, a shield from dark,
An ember bright, eternal spark.

In shadows deep, one flame remains,
Through winds and storms, it keeps its reigns,
A beacon through night's endless night,
Defying odds, with fiery might.

Each flicker tells a tale of old,
Of love and hope in hearts of gold,
Through every age, it stands the test,
In every soul, this fire's blessed.

Against the cold of worldly skies,
It softly whispers and defies,
A constant light, forever tame,
United hearts, an eternal flame.

Destiny's Tapestry

Threads of fate in colors vast,
Weave a story, shadows cast,
A pattern bold of joy and pain,
Each stitch a moment, love's refrain.

Through highs and lows, the fabric weaves,
In whispered secrets time retrieves,
Each strand a glimpse of destiny,
An artwork formed, so endlessly.

In golden threads that shimmer bright,
Lie dreams and hopes, a guiding light,
Woven deep within this frame,
An ever-changing, vibrant flame.

From knots of sorrow, frayed and torn,
To patches mended, newly worn,
A masterpiece in every hue,
Destiny's design, steadfast and true.

Heartbeats in Sync

Two lives entwined with gentle grace,
Across the years, their paths embrace,
In rhythm sweet, their heartbeats play,
A love that grows with each new day.

In silence shared and in the light,
They find their peace, their spirits right,
A dance of souls in perfect tune,
Under the glowing silver moon.

Trials they face with hands held tight,
Through storm and calm, they share the night,
Together strong, they rise above,
In harmony, they sing of love.

With every beat, their promise keeps,
In waking hours, in tranquil sleeps,
A bond that time cannot unlink,
Forever more, heartbeats in sync.

Twin Souls

In the quiet moonlit night,
Two hearts beat as one, so right,
Bound by threads unseen, yet tight,
Twin souls in the endless flight.

Through the storms and past the pain,
Hand in hand, where love does reign,
Eternal dance on life's terrain,
Twin souls, a love so plain.

Eyes that lock in timeless gaze,
A connection, a passionate blaze,
Together in a dreamy haze,
Twin souls in love's sweet maze.

With every whispered word and sigh,
They share a bond, and up they fly,
Upon love's wings, reaching the sky,
Twin souls, never to say goodbye.

In the journey of life's grand role,
Together they heal and make whole,
Two souls merged into a single goal,
Eternal love, their story told.

Perfect Harmony

In the dawn's first golden light,
Hearts align, a pure delight,
Symphony of love so bright,
Perfect harmony takes flight.

Each note played with tender care,
A melody beyond compare,
Love's sweet song floats through the air,
In harmony, a perfect pair.

With a touch, the music grows,
A rhythm that the heart well knows,
Everlasting, love's echo flows,
In harmony, the passion shows.

In the laughter and the tears,
Through the trials and the years,
Together facing all their fears,
Perfect harmony endears.

In each other's arms they find,
A concert of the heart and mind,
In this love, forever bind,
Perfect harmony, intertwined.

Unified Beat

Two hearts drum in unified beat,
A rhythm strong, pure and sweet,
In each other, they complete,
A love that time cannot defeat.

Through the silence, through the noise,
Love's true echo, gentle poise,
Every moment, it enjoys,
Unified beat with endless joys.

Hand in hand, through life's dance,
Both enraptured in the trance,
Unified beat, it does enhance,
Love's story in a timeless glance.

In each pulse, in every find,
In their dreams, their lives unwind,
Hearts united, closely bind,
Unified beat of one kind.

Together through the highs and lows,
Love's rhythm ever steadily grows,
In their hearts forever glows,
Unified beat, love's true prose.

Love's Resonance

In the whispers soft and low,
In the way the breezes blow,
There's a resonance, a glow,
A love that the stars bestow.

Through the echoes of their laughter,
In the moments they are after,
Love's resonance, a living chapter,
Ever after, thereafter.

In the silence of the night,
In the dawn's first gentle light,
Love's resonance takes its flight,
Guiding through life's delight.

With a gaze, their souls do meet,
In each other, life's complete,
Love's resonance in heartbeat,
Together, love's retreat.

In their world, a sacred sound,
Where true happiness is found,
Love's resonance all around,
In this song, they are bound.

Eternal Voyage

Upon the seas of twilight gray,
We set our sails anew;
Through storms and calm, by night and day,
Our journey we pursue.

Stars above, a guiding light,
Reflections on the deep;
In whispered winds, a silent flight,
Both wakeful and in sleep.

With every crest, our spirits rise,
A dance upon the wave;
Beneath the vast and endless skies,
Our hearts together brave.

Horizons stretch to realms unknown,
A mystery to unfold;
In every tide, a promise shown,
A story yet untold.

This voyage, an eternal quest,
In love, we find our way;
Together bound, forever blessed,
By night and by the day.

Sacred Union

In sacred moments, hearts entwine,
A bond both pure and true;
Two souls connected, love divine,
In all they say and do.

With every touch, a silent vow,
To cherish and to hold;
Together through the here and now,
And as our lives unfold.

A tapestry of golden threads,
Woven through our days;
A deeper meaning, gently spreads,
In countless, tender ways.

Where once were two, now only one,
A unity so bright;
It shines beneath the morning sun,
And in the quiet night.

In sacred union, we remain,
Though trials may arise;
Our love, a never-ending flame,
Reflected in our eyes.

Twin Flames of Eternity

Twin flames that dance in cosmic fire,
In synchronicity;
A love that lifts us ever higher,
Through endless mystery.

From ancient realms, our spirits blend,
A bond of ageless force;
Together through time's gentle bend,
We chart a destined course.

In mirrored gaze, we see our souls,
A perfect symmetry;
Entwined in dreams, as seasons roll,
In timeless harmony.

Though shadows form and winds may blow,
Our light will not deter;
For in this love, we truly know,
Eternity's sweet blur.

Twin flames forever, hearts combined,
In realms both near and far;
A love transcendent and divine,
Guided by a shared star.

Fusion of Hearts

Two hearts that beat in perfect time,
A symphony of grace;
In every word, a gentle rhyme,
Together we embrace.

With each new dawn, our spirits soar,
A dance upon the breeze;
In love, we find an open door,
A path that none can seize.

The fusion of our hopes and dreams,
A tapestry so grand;
In every look, a secret gleams,
And love, our guiding hand.

Though worlds may shift and seasons change,
Our bond remains the same;
In laughter bright or moments strange,
We call the other's name.

In fusion's glow, we walk as one,
A journey just begun;
Together till our days are done,
Our love, a setting sun.

Milton Keynes UK
Ingram Content Group UK Ltd.
UKHW020116070624
443692UK00004B/88

9 789916 860045